RAILWAYS AND TRANSPORT SAFETY ACT 2003

EXPLANATORY NOTES

INTRODUCTION

1.   These Explanatory Notes relate to the Railways and Transport Safety Act 2003. They have been prepared by the Department for Transport in order to assist the reader in understanding the Act. They do not form part of the Act, and have not been endorsed by Parliament.

2.   The Notes need to be read in conjunction with the Act. They are not, and are not meant to be, a comprehensive description of the Act. So where a section or part of a section does not seem to require any explanation or comment, none is given.

SUMMARY

3.   The Act creates an independent body tasked with establishing the causes of accidents on the railways. This body, which would be called the Rail Accident Investigation Branch, would be established on a similar model to that which already exists in the marine and aviation sectors. The establishment of this new body is in response to recommendations made in September 2001 by Part 2 of Lord Cullen's Report into the Ladbroke Grove rail crash.

4.   The Act provides for a Regulatory Board to replace the Rail Regulator, in line with standard practice for the regulation of utilities.

5.   The Act creates a police authority for the British Transport Police Force ("BTP"), transferring responsibility for the BTP from the Strategic Rail Authority ("SRA") and existing BTP Committee to the new police authority. It also gives the BTP a wholly statutory, rather than part-statutory and part-contractual, jurisdiction over the railways.

6.   The Act introduces alcohol limits and related measures for crews on water-borne vessels and certain aviation personnel, that broadly replicates drink/driving legislation already applying to motorists and certain railway workers.

7.   The Act also contains a miscellaneous section, which makes provision for measures including:

- incorporation into UK law of a modification to the 1999 International Convention concerning Carriage by Rail (COTIF). The new Convention text takes account of the major changes in management of railway operations in many countries, in particular increasing separation of train operations from infrastructure management, and the introduction of open access rights, allowing for the possibility of more than one operator on any one network.

- powers to create a levy on the rail industry, to meet the expenses of the Health and Safety Executive (HSE) as regards railway systems.

- powers to ensure that persons subject to directions by the Secretary of State under the Aviation & Maritime Security Act 1990, or instructions under the Railways Act 1993, may only contract out security work to companies figuring on a list held by the Secretary of State.

- a duty on highway authorities to remove ice and snow from roads for which they are responsible.

- amendments to the Greater London Authority Act 1999 to remedy certain unintended consequences it would otherwise have had for the transfer of London Underground to Transport for London.

8.   The Act is in seven Parts, with 8 Schedules:

- Part 1: (Investigation of Railway Accidents)
- Part 2: (Office of Rail Regulation)
- Part 3: (British Transport Police)
- Part 4: (Shipping: Alcohol and Drugs)
- Part 5: (Aviation: Alcohol and Drugs)
- Part 6: (Miscellaneous)
- Part 7: (General)

TERRITORIAL EXTENT

9.   This Act extends to the whole of the United Kingdom, with the following exceptions:

Scotland

10.   The Act extends to Scotland except:

- Part 1 (Investigation of Railway Accidents) in so far as it applies to tramways
- Part 3 (British Transport Police) in so far as it applies to tramways
- Section 28 (Exercise of powers by civilians)
- Section 86 (Shipping: right of entry)
- Section 98 (Aviation: right of entry)
- Section 109 (Road traffic: fixed penalty)
- Section 111 (Highways: snow and ice)

Northern Ireland

11.   The Act extends to Northern Ireland except:

- Part 2 (Office of Rail Regulation)
- Part 3 (British Transport Police)
- Section 104 (Office of Rail Regulation: general duties)
- Section 105 (Railways safety levy)
- Section 106 (Railway security services)
- Section 107 and Schedule 7 (Road Traffic: testing for drink and drugs)
- Section 108 (Traffic regulation on long distance routes)
- Section 109 (Road traffic: fixed penalty)
- Section 110 (Seat belts: delivery drivers)
- Section 111 (Highways: snow and ice)
- Section 114 (Railways in London: transfers)
- Section 115 (Railways in London: information)

Territorial application: Wales

12.   This Act does not affect any of the National Assembly of Wales's powers. However, section 111 will impose a duty on the National Assembly to remove snow and ice from those highways for which it has responsibility.

THE ACT

Part 1 - Investigation of Railway Accidents

13.   This Part extends to England, Wales and Northern Ireland. It also extends to Scotland except in so far as it applies to tramways.

Background

14.   Railways are statistically one of the safest means of transportation. Travel by rail is 6 times safer than travel by car.[1] However, in recent years, a number of serious accidents on the railways have affected public confidence and have revealed weaknesses in safety regulation.

---

[1] Transport Statistics 2002 – DfT

15.   On 5 October 1999, at Ladbroke Grove Junction, about 2 miles west of Paddington Station there was a head-on crash at high speed between two trains. This caused the death of 31 people, including both train drivers, and inflicted injuries, some of them critical, on over 400 other people.

16.   As a consequence of this crash, Lord Cullen was appointed by the Health and Safety Commission (HSC), with the consent of the Deputy Prime Minister, to conduct a Public Inquiry under Section 14(2)(b) of the Health and Safety at Work etc Act 1974. Lord Cullen's terms of reference were:

"1) To inquire into, and draw lessons from, the accident near Paddington Station on 5 October 1999, taking account of the findings of the Health and Safety Executive's investigations into immediate causes.

2) To consider general experience derived from relevant accidents on the railway since the Hidden Inquiry [into the 1988 Clapham rail crash], with a view to drawing conclusions about:

   a) factors which affect safety management
   b) the appropriateness of the current regulatory regime.

3) In the light of the above, to make recommendations for improving safety on the future railway."

17.   Lord Cullen's inquiry reported in 2 parts, the second of which looked at rail safety management and regulation. Lord Cullen's Part 2 Report[2] made 74 recommendations which the Secretary of State asked the HSC to ensure were acted upon and implemented. 17 of these concerned accident investigation, including the creation of an independent Rail Accident Investigation Branch (RAIB), with appropriate powers and duties. Some applied solely to industry investigations and inquiries.

Commentary on sections

18.   Part 1 of this Act implements certain key recommendations made by Lord Cullen in his Ladbroke Grove Part 2 Report. This Part makes provision for the creation of an independent body of rail accident inspectors known as the Rail Accident Investigation Branch (RAIB), which will (as with the air and marine accident investigation branches) form part of the Department for Transport. The fundamental purpose of the RAIB will be to undertake investigations, openly and transparently, which look for the root causes of accidents and incidents without apportioning blame. It will have no prosecution function. The RAIB will conduct investigations on the railways following accidents or incidents. RAIB inspectors will have the power to enter all railway property, land adjoining railway property and certain other places connected to the accident or incident if they think that there may be evidence relevant to the investigation. If asked, they will have to show their identification before they can enter such places.

19.   The provisions:

  •   Establish the RAIB, charging it with investigating the causes of railway accidents and incidents with a view to learning lessons and fostering a safer railway;

---

[2] The Ladbroke Grove Rail Inquiry, Part 2 Report, Health and Safety Commission, London, September 2001

- Give RAIB inspectors the powers they need to conduct investigations and to require the disclosure of evidence related to these investigations;

- Make it an offence to not comply with a requirement made by an RAIB inspector, or knowingly to provide inaccurate or misleading information to an inspector without reasonable excuse; and

- Allow the Secretary of State to make regulations about how the RAIB is to conduct its investigations, the form and content of RAIB reports, and on measures the RAIB is to take before publishing its reports.

Section 1: Meaning of "railway" and "railway property"

20.   Section 1 defines "railway" in this Part as a railway or tramway within the meaning given by section 67(1) of the Transport & Works Act 1992. In that section:

- "railway" means:

"a system of transport employing parallel rails which—
    (a) provide support and guidance for vehicles carried on flanged wheels, and
    (b) form a track which either is of a gauge of at least 350 millimetres or crosses a carriageway (whether or not on the same level),
but does not include a tramway."

- "tramway" means:

"a system of transport used wholly or mainly for the carriage of passengers employing parallel rails which—
    (a) provide support and guidance for vehicles carried on flanged wheels, and
    (b) are laid wholly or mainly along a street or in any other place to which the public has access (including a place to which the public has access only on making a payment)."

21.   "Railway property" is also defined.

Section 2: Meaning of "railway accident" and "railway incident"

22.   Section 2 defines a railway accident or incident as an accident or incident that occurs on railway property and is or may be relevant to the operation of the railway. It also allows the Secretary of State to make regulations about what may or may not be treated as such an accident or incident or when an accident will be treated as serious

23.   Regulations made under section 2(2) may detail the circumstances when an accident or incident would be relevant to the operation of the railway. Accidents or incidents which are not of relevance to the operation of the railway may not be investigated by the RAIB. Such incidents might include, for example, a minor fire in a railway station shop, or where a person trips over on a railway station concourse.

24.   Section 2(3) makes clear that regulations may specify whether accidents in particular locations would be investigated by the RAIB. It is intended to use this power to provide for the particular circumstances of the Channel Tunnel, which is bi-nationally regulated through the Channel Tunnel Intergovernmental Commission. The Channel Tunnel Safety Authority has primary responsibility for investigating safety-related incidents in the Channel Tunnel. It is intended to make regulations under section 2(3) to ensure that should the

Intergovernmental Commission or Safety Authority ask the RAIB to undertake any investigations within the Tunnel, it would have the power to do so.

Section 3: Establishment

25.   Section 3 establishes the RAIB, broadly along models already existing for the Air Accident Investigation Branch (AAIB) (established in regulations made under section 75 of the Civil Aviation Act 1982), and the Marine Accident Investigation Branch (MAIB) (established under section 267 of the Merchant Shipping Act 1995).

Section 4: General Aims

26.   Section 4 establishes that the fundamental aims of the RAIB will be to improve the safety of railways and prevent railway accidents and railway incidents.

Section 5: Assistance to others

27.   Section 5 will permit the Chief Inspector of Rail Accidents to arrange for the RAIB to provide its services to third parties. This might include, for example, assisting the accident investigation body of another country, particularly if there might be safety lessons for the UK railway. The Chief Inspector may charge for the RAIB's services if he or she considers it appropriate.

Section 6: Annual Report

28.   Section 6 requires the Secretary of State to make regulations requiring the Chief Inspector of Rail Accidents to produce an Annual Report. This report would include details of safety recommendations made by RAIB in that year and set out the action taken by the rail industry to implement those recommendations.

Section 7: Investigations

29.   Section 7 makes provision as to the railway accidents or incidents that the RAIB is to investigate.

- Subsection (1)(a) requires the RAIB to investigate serious accidents. Subsection (1)(b) provides the RAIB with discretion as to whether or not to investigate non- serious accidents or any incident. Subsection 1(c) provides that the RAIB is also to investigate non-serious accidents or incidents, if it is required to by regulations made by the Secretary of State.

- Subsection (2), however, provides for the Chief Inspector of Rail Accidents to exercise discretion when considering whether or not to investigate a serious accident on a tramway. Although accidents and incidents affecting tramways fall within the remit of the RAIB, the effect of section 7(2) gives the Chief Inspector discretion as to whether or not to investigate tramway accidents. This is because tramways run in various types of alignment, on street, alongside a highway, or off street. The investigation of an accident affecting a road-running part of a tramway would fall normally to the police to investigate whilst an accident affecting an off-street running part of a tramway would normally be investigated by the RAIB.

- Subsections (3) and (5) when taken together make clear that the RAIB is to try to work out the cause of the accident, without apportioning blame or liability. Although it will not consider blame or liability, the RAIB will publish a report setting out the cause even if blame or liability may be inferred as a result. These provisions are equivalent to those existing for the AAIB in regulation 4 of the Civil Aviation (Investigation of Air Accidents and Incidents) Regulations 1996, and for the MAIB in regulation 4 of the Merchant Shipping (Accident Investigation and Reporting) Regulations 1999.

Section 8: Investigator's powers

30.   Section 8 gives RAIB inspectors the powers necessary to conduct an investigation. These provisions are modelled on the powers available to AAIB and MAIB accident investigators.

31.   Subsection (3) creates new offences, designed to prevent RAIB inspectors from being hindered in their investigations. For example it is to be an offence for a person to fail to comply, without a reasonable excuse, with a requirement made by an inspector or to provide an inspector with evidence that person knows or suspects to be misleading. A person will also be committing an offence if he obstructs a person who is accompanying the inspector and who has been authorised to do so by the Chief Inspector of Rail Accidents.

32.   Subsections (5) and (6) give the RAIB primacy in an investigation. This is to ensure that while the different parties involved in investigating an accident will work alongside each other, one body, the RAIB, is to be in the lead. This provision clarifies that where a person (such as a police officer or any other investigator) seeks to take a particular course of action during an investigation, the Chief Inspector of Rail Accidents, or a person acting on his behalf, is able to make the decision on whether that course of action may be taken.

Section 9: Regulations

33.   Section 9(1) gives the Secretary of State the power to make regulations about the way in which the RAIB is to conduct its investigations. Subsection (2) provides that those regulations can also make requirements about the RAIB reports.

34.   Subsections (2)(d) and (2)(e) allow regulations to be made which could require the RAIB to ensure that its reports are not made public until any person or organisation whose reputation may be adversely affected by the report is given the opportunity to make representations on that draft report .

35.   Subsection (4) would permit regulations to make provision on how and whether information held by the RAIB could be disclosed to third parties. It is expected for example, that the regulations will provide that no witness statement given to the RAIB may be disclosed to a third party (such as, but not limited to, the police or the Health and Safety Executive (HSE)) unless the witness himself releases it, or unless a court orders its disclosure.

36.   Non-statutory provision will be made for prosecuting authorities to be given the details of those who have given statements to the RAIB.

Section 10: Requirement to Investigate

37.   Section 10 provides for the Chief Inspector of Rail Accidents to direct whether an accident or incident on railway property will be investigated and how an accident or incident must be investigated. These directions will be to those in the railway industry, that means that directions may be made to the manager or controller of railway property and to all those who participate in the management or control of railway property. It will be an offence to fail to comply with such a direction.

Section 11: Accident regulations

38.   Section 11 allows the Secretary of State to make regulations which would allow, for example, requirements to be made about the reporting of accidents and incidents to the RAIB (so that they may then investigate those accidents and incidents). Such provision would not affect existing obligations to report accidents to HSE.

Public Sector financial and manpower cost

39.   The additional staffing numbers needed by the Department for Transport for the Rail Accident Investigation Branch are identified in Table 1 of the Regulatory Impact Assessment. This anticipates 14 professional staff and 8 support staff. Applying average gross wage rates by grade, plus an allowance for non-wage labour costs, the annual staffing costs of the RAIB would be around £1.3 million. Running and other costs for RAIB would add up to about £550,000 such that total annual costs for the RAIB would be about £1.85 million (Table 3). Over a ten-year period the discounted present cost would be about £14 million.

Human Rights assessment

40.   The RAIB provisions of this Act, and those matters that will be included in regulations made under a power in this Act, have been considered for their compatibility with the European Convention of Human Rights. Although certain aspects of RAIB provisions engage rights protected by the ECHR, the Government considers that these may be justified.

41.   RAIB inspectors will have the power to enter any land for the purposes of conducting an investigation into a railway accident or incident. The exercise of this power could interfere with a person's right to respect for a private and family life or home (protected by Article 8) or could interfere with a person's peaceful enjoyment of their possessions (protected by Article 1 of the First Protocol). However, even if these rights were interfered with, the Government considers such interference justified on the grounds that this statutory power is necessary to ensure public safety on the railways; and it is in the general public interest that such investigations take place.

42.   To assist RAIB in working to improve safety on the railways, it is important that

people feel that they can talk freely to RAIB inspectors, without fear that what they say might be used against them in another way (such as legal proceedings). With this in mind, it is intended that regulations made under section 9 will provide that statements obtained by RAIB inspectors may only be disclosed to a third party (such as a prosecutor) if a court orders that such disclosure is in the public interest, or if the person who has made the statement release it themselves. This will go towards bolstering the existing protection already afforded by Article 6 of the ECHR.

Part 2 - Office of Rail Regulation

43.   This part extends to England, Wales and Scotland.

Background

44.   The post of Rail Regulator was created as part of the privatisation of the railways, with his functions defined in the Railways Act 1993, as amended by the Transport Act 2000. This part of the Act, together with Schedules 1, 2 and 3, replaces the Rail Regulator with a corporate body established along board lines, called the Office of Rail Regulation.   The Office assumes all of the existing functions of the Regulator.

45.   The Secretary of State for Transport announced the decision to introduce a regulatory board structure for rail regulation on 12 June 2002.   This move is consistent with the recommendations of the Better Regulation Task Force report on economic regulators (July 2001), and follows what has been done or is in the process of being done for other regulators. A public consultation document entitled "Creating a Regulatory Board for Railways" was subsequently issued.

Commentary on sections

Section 15: Establishment & Schedule 1: Office of Rail Regulation

46.   Section 15(2) gives effect to Schedule 1. Schedule 1 gives details about the membership, staff and financial arrangements of the new Office of Rail Regulation.

47.   Paragraphs 6 and 7 allow the Office to establish committees and to delegate its functions to such committees.   Membership of those committees is not limited to Office members and employees. This enables the Office to bring outside expertise to committees, which may be advisory or decision making and deal with specific tasks or have continuing functions.

48.   Paragraph 18 requires the Office to make arrangements to manage potential or perceived conflicts of interests which could affect the performance of a particular function and, as well as members, covers employees and others appointed to committees.

- Paragraph 18(1) requires declaration and withdrawal from involvement where a financial or other personal interest is likely to influence a person's performance of a particular function.

- Paragraph 18(2) applies where an interest is not in fact likely to influence a person's performance of the function, but which is nonetheless relevant to that function. In such a case, the interest must be declared and the person must not perform that function, unless the Office decides that he may do so.

Section 16: Transfer of functions

49.   Section 16(5) gives effect to Schedule 2. This Schedule makes consequential amendments to existing legislation as a result of the transfer from the Rail Regulator to the Office of Rail Regulation.

50.   Section 16(5) also gives effect to Schedule 3. This Schedule provides, amongst other things, for actions of the Regulator prior to commencement to continue to be valid.

Schedule 2 – Abolition of Rail Regulator: consequential amendments

51.   This Schedule amends legislation so that existing references to the Regulator will be substituted with references to the Office of Rail Regulation and includes related minor drafting changes.

Schedule 3 – Abolition of Rail Regulator: savings, etc.

52.   The effect of this Schedule is that anything done by the Regulator prior to the transfer of his functions to the Office of Rail Regulation will continue to be valid as if it had been done by the Office. Similarly, anything in the process of being done by, or in relation to, the Regulator will be continued by, or in relation to, the Office.

53.   Paragraph 6 makes it clear that the Act does not affect the International Rail Regulator in any way. That is a separate office, which will continue to exist.

Public Sector financial and manpower cost

54.   The appointment of additional non-executive members of a Regulatory Board for the Office of Rail Regulation will entail additional costs. This would be recovered at least in part from the regulated industry, though offset indirectly by increases in public subsidy. The extra costs would probably be less than £200,000, less than a 1.5% increase in the ORR's budget.

Human Rights assessment

55.   The Government considers that the substitution of a regulatory board of rail regulation for the Rail Regulator does not involve any human rights implications, and that the provisions of the Act concerning the Office of Rail Regulation are compatible with the Convention.

Part 3 – British Transport Police

56.   The British Transport Police Force ("BTP") operates in England, Scotland and Wales but not in Northern Ireland. Accordingly this part extends to England, Wales and Scotland

(except in so far as it applies to tramways and the exercise of powers by civilians).

Background

57.   The BTP is the national police force for the railways in Great Britain. The force is also responsible for policing London Underground, the Docklands Light Railway, Croydon Tramlink and the Midland Metro. Their main activities include law and order policing, maintaining the Queen's peace and protecting staff and the public on the railways. The force deals with all crimes, including murder, violence, sexual offences, robberies, thefts and fraud, and a host of other railway specific incidents, such as accidents, fatalities and suicides. In particular the force has expertise in anti-terrorist strategy, handling of major incidents and the policing of travelling sports fans.

58.   The BTP has its origins in the police forces of the many railway companies established by various Acts of Parliament in the 19th century. After the Second World War, nationalisation brought the different railway police forces together under the control of the British Railways Board ("BRB"). BTP constables are currently employed by the Strategic Rail Authority ("SRA") as successor to the BRB and are overseen by the BTP Committee whose principal function is to provide an adequate and efficient police service for the railways. The BTP Committee, in effect, performs many of the functions of a Home Office police authority.

59.   In October 2001 the Government issued a consultation document entitled 'Modernising the British Transport Police' with detailed proposals to bring BTP into line with Home Office police forces in terms of accountability, status and powers. The Government's main proposals in the consultation document were:

- to establish a police Authority for the BTP;

- to place the jurisdiction of BTP constables over the railways on a statutory basis;

- to give BTP constables jurisdiction outside the railways in certain circumstances; and

- to give BTP constables a number of additional police powers that were only available to constables of local police forces.

60.   The proposal to give BTP constables jurisdiction outside the railways was taken forward in section 100 of the Anti-terrorism, Crime & Security Act 2001. Schedule 7 of that Act, and sections 75 and 76 of the subsequent Police Reform Act 2002, extended to the BTP the additional police powers included in the consultation document. The remaining proposals, namely the establishment of a police authority and giving the BTP a statutory jurisdiction over the railways, are included in this Act.

61.   The existing staff of the BTP (both constables and the civilian staff) will be transferred to the new Authority under the provisions of the Act. Staff terms of employment, including pension benefits, will not be affected by the transfer to the Authority.

Commentary on Sections

62.   The BTP Authority ("the Authority") is to be modelled on existing Home Office police authorities (such as Northamptonshire Police Authority) with the sections in this part of the Act largely mirroring the Police Act 1996 provisions on such authorities. Where the sections do not mirror the Police Act 1996 provisions in every respect, this is generally only so as to meet the specific circumstances of the BTP as a national police force for the railways, as opposed to a county or metropolitan force.

63.   The following table details the sections that are based on provisions in the Police Act 1996, or other legislation where appropriate.

Section	Description of section	Section of Police Act 1996 that provision is based upon (or other Act where appropriate)
18	Establishment of the Authority	Section 3
19	Exercise of functions	Section 6
20	Establishment of police force	Sections 2 and 6
21	Chief Constable; appointment, functions and power to make regulations for removal and suspension.	Sections 11 and 42
22	Deputy Chief Constable; appointment, delegation of Chief Constable's powers and regulations for removal and suspension	Sections 11A and 12A
23	Assistant Chief Constables; appointment, delegation of Chief Constable's powers and regulations for removal and suspension	Sections 12 and 12A
24	Employment, control and attestation of constables	Section 29
25	Employment, control and attestation of special constables	Section 27
25(5)	Liability for wrongful acts of special constables	Section 88
26	Employment and control of police cadets	Section 28
27	Employment and control of civilian employees of the police authority	Section 15
28	Exercise of powers by civilians	Sections 38, 39, 42, 45, 46, 47 and Schedule 4 Police Reform Act 2002
30	Trade union membership	Section 64
31	Jurisdiction of constables	Section 30

Section	Description of section	Section of Police Act 1996 that provision is based upon (or other Act where appropriate)
33	Police services agreements	Section 132(3), Railways Act 1993
35	Arbitration of disputes by the Secretary of State	Section 132(4), Railways Act 1993
36	Authority regulations for BTP officers	Section 50
36 (2)	Authority regulations for disciplinary proceedings and appeal matters	Sections 84 and 85
37	Authority regulations for special constables	Section 51
38	Authority regulations for police cadets	Section 52
39	Establishment and regulations for the BTP Federation	Sections 59 and 60
42	Secretary of State regulations for the BTP	Sections 50, 51, 52 and 60
43	Secretary of State regulations on disciplinary proceedings and appeal matters	Sections 84 and 85
44	Secretary of State regulations on BTP equipment	Section 53
45	Secretary of State regulations on procedure and practice	Section 53A
46	Conditions of service: BTP Conference	Section 133, Railways Act 1993
47	Code of practice for the Authority	Section 39
48	Code of practice for the Chief Constable	Section 39A
49	Service outside the Police Force	Section 97
50	Authority's policing objectives	Section 7
51	Direction to Authority on policing objectives	Section 37
52	Railways policing plan	Section 8
53	Performance targets	Section 38
55	Three-year strategy plans	Section 6A
56	Reports by the Chief Constable	Section 22
57	Annual report by the Authority	Section 9
58	Other reports to the Secretary of State	Sections 43 and 44
59	Police statistics	Section 45
60 and 61	Inquiries	Section 34 Police Act 1997
62	Public consultation	Section 96
63	Inspection of the police force and publication of reports	Sections 54 and 55

Section	Description of section	Section of Police Act 1996 that provision is based upon (or other Act where appropriate)
64, 65 and 66	Actions after adverse inspection reports, remedial direction and action plan	Sections 40, 41A and 41B
67	Senior appointment: delegation of Secretary of State functions to the Chief Inspector of Constabulary	Section 54(3A)
68	Offences: assault and impersonation of a constable	Sections 89 and 90
70	International assistance	Section 26
71	Exercise of functions by the Secretary of State	Section 36

Schedule 4, Paragraph	Description of Provision	Section of Police Act 1996 that provision is based upon (or other Act where appropriate)
1 and 2	Appointment of members	Section 4 and Schedule 2, paragraph 1
3	Tenure of members	Schedule 2, paragraph 15
4 and 5	Chairman and deputy chairman	Schedule 2, paragraphs 9 and 9A
7	Disqualification of members	Schedule 2, paragraph 11 and 14
9	Code of practice for standards of conduct for members	Section 50 of the Local Government Act 2000
10	Staff of the Authority	Section 15
11	Appointment of Treasurer	Section 112 of the Local Government Finance Act 1988
11	Appointment of Clerk	Section 16 and Section 4 of the Local Government and Housing Act 1989
15	Validity of proceedings	Schedule 2, paragraph 23 and 24
16, 17 and 18	BTP Fund and Accounts	Section 14
19	BTP Budget	Section 19
21	Members' remuneration, allowances etc	Schedule 2, paragraph 25A
23(2)	Payment for liability of wrongful acts of constables	Section 88
23 (3)	Rewards for diligence	Section 31

Schedule 4, Paragraph	Description of Provision	Section of Police Act 1996 that provision is based upon (or other Act where appropriate)
28	Acceptance of grants, loans and other payments	Section 93

Section 18 & Schedule 4: The British Transport Police Authority

64.   Section 18 gives effect to Schedule 4. This Schedule deals with membership of the Authority and contains requirements about its proceedings and details about financial matters, including remuneration and pension arrangements.

Membership of the Police Authority

65.   The Secretary of State will be responsible for appointing the members of the Authority, including the chairman and vice-chairman. It is envisaged that the Authority will normally consist of 13 members. Paragraph 1 restricts the number of members between 11 and 17, although the Secretary of State may by order change these numbers after consulting with the Authority.   Paragraph 2 provides that the Authority's membership should include persons who can provide knowledge and experience of the issues that concern passengers, the railways industry, railways employees and the regions.

Pensions

66.   Paragraphs 24 to 26 make provision in relation to pensions. Paragraph 24 enables the Secretary of State to make amendments to the occupational pension scheme for constables of the Authority. The scope of amendments would be limited. The provision intends to enable amendment of the trust documentation for the scheme, to recognise the new status of the Authority and its relationship with the Secretary of State, but not to provide for changing the pension benefit structure or winding up the scheme. Any amendments, on which there would be prior consultation with the scheme trustees, would be consistent with the members' historic protected rights under Schedule 11 to the Railways Act 1993.

67.   Paragraph 25 enables the Authority, with the Secretary of State's consent, to set up new arrangements to provide for retirement benefits for staff.

Sections 21-26: Senior officers and constables of the BTP

68.   Sections 21 (Chief Constable), 22 (Deputy Chief Constable), 23 (Assistant Chief Constables), 24 (constables), 25 (special constables) and 26 (cadets) make provision so that the BTP will have the same ranks as Home Office police forces under the Police Act 1996. These sections also provide that these officers' functions, appointments and other associated matters are to be based on the provisions of the Police Act 1996.

69.   Only where necessary to meet the specific needs of the BTP do the provisions in the Act differ from the Police Act 1996. Provision made by regulations under the Act will have to follow the Police Act 1996, and any   regulations made under that Act.   The

BTP regulations can only make different provision to meet the specific circumstances of the BTP. This means that should the Secretary of State make regulations regarding the suspension and removal of the senior officers of the BTP, then such regulations would seek to replicate the existing provisions in the Police Act 1996, any regulations made under that Act and only differ to take account of any specific needs of the BTP.

70.   A BTP constable or special constable appointed under section 24 or 25 need only be appointed in England & Wales or in Scotland to be considered a constable throughout Great Britain.

71.   Section 25(5) covers liability for the wrongful acts of BTP special constables when on BTP business. Special constables, unlike constables, are not employees of the Authority, and liability does not fall on the Authority via their employer's contractual responsibility. The section provides that liability for any wrongful acts committed by BTP special constables in the course of their duties rests with the Chief Constable. The section also allows the Chief Constable to pay out of the BTP Fund any damages or costs arising from this conduct.

Section 28: Exercise of powers by civilians

72.   Section 28 provides that the provisions of the Police Reform Act 2002 that relate to police powers and duties conferred on civilians shall apply to the BTP. As a result the Chief Constable will be able to designate suitably skilled and trained employees of the Authority who are under his direction and control as different types of civilian officers with certain powers and duties. The powers and duties are detailed in Schedule 4 to the Police Reform Act 2002. Such civilians can be designated as: community support officers; investigating officers; detention officers; and escort officers.

73.   Powers which can be conferred on community support officers include the power to issue a range of fixed penalty notices relating to anti-social behaviour; the power to request a name and address from a person committing a fixed-penalty offence or behaving in an anti-social manner; and the power to detain, for a limited period awaiting the arrival of a constable, a person who fails to comply with the request to give their name and address.

74.   Powers which can be conferred on investigating officers include those that would be needed to support the work of civilian investigating officers in specialist areas, such as financial crime, and are mainly linked to entry, search and seizure. They include the right to apply for and be granted search warrants under the Police and Criminal Evidence Act 1984; and the power to execute warrants, to enter property and to seize and retain things for which a search has been authorised.

75.   Powers which can be conferred on detention officers include the power to require defined categories of persons to attend a police station to have their fingerprints taken; the power to carry out non-intimate searches of persons detained at police stations and to seize items found during such searches; and the power to carry out intimate searches in the same limited circumstances that are applicable to constables.

76.   Powers which can be conferred on escort officers include the power to transport

arrested persons to police stations, and between a police station and another location specified by the custody officer. An escort officer can also be placed under a duty to prevent a detainee's escape.

77. By virtue of section 28(2)(f), civilians designated by the Chief Constable will be able to carry out their functions in any place in England and Wales where a BTP constable has jurisdiction under section 31(a) - (f). This includes, but is not limited to, railway stations and track. They will also be able to operate outside the railways elsewhere in England and Wales if the matter is connected to the railways.

Section 29: Terms of employment

78. Section 29 is designed to ensure that the Authority's employment practices fall within the criteria set by the Secretary of State. The BTP's officers will hold the office of constable and also be employees of the Authority. In transferring their employment from the SRA to the Authority their existing terms and conditions of employment will be protected. Thus far the Secretary of State has retained an overarching control on BTP constables' and civilians' pay through the SRA's financial framework. This section will enable the Secretary of State to ensure that the Authority maintains pay parity for BTP constables and civilians with their Home Office colleagues.

Section 31: Jurisdiction

79. The BTP's main duties consist of public policing, exactly like a Home Office police force. However, unlike a Home Office force, almost all of the BTP's duties, and in particular its routine patrols, occur on private property, albeit property to which the public may have access i.e. railway stations and trains. The BTP's existing jurisdiction on this private property flows from a combination of a 1949 private Act of Parliament[3] and numerous private agreements between the SRA and the railway companies. Most operators of railway vehicles and certain railway assets are required under the Railways Act 1993 to have a licence. It is a condition of those licences that the operator must enter in to an agreement with the SRA to engage the services of the BTP on its property. It is these agreements, combined with the 1949 Act that gives the BTP the right to police most railway property.

80. Section 31 gives the BTP a wholly statutory railway jurisdiction throughout England, Scotland and Wales. Within this jurisdiction a BTP constable has the powers and privileges of a Home Office constable. The jurisdiction extends over all railway property. It also extends outside railway property (a town high street for example) throughout Great Britain in relation to railway matters. This jurisdiction would, for example, allow a BTP constable to pursue a person who commits an offence on the railways but then absconds from railway property.

81. In order to allow the BTP to police railway property on a day-to-day basis, section 31(2) & (3) gives the BTP constable a statutory right to enter and police certain defined areas of railway property.

---

[3] Section 53 of The British Transport Commission Act 1949

82.   On property not listed in section 31(3), the BTP constable is subject to the same restrictions that apply to a Home Office constable. In particular, an officer would be unable to enter private property unless invited, holding a warrant, or exercising some other right of entry (in another Act of Parliament for example).

Section 32: Prosecution

83.   Normally prosecutions for most criminal cases investigated by the BTP are referred to the Crown Prosecution Service.   However the BTP does prosecute minor offences particularly those under the railway bye-laws and minor road traffic violations.   This section allows for this to continue.

Sections 33-35: Police Services Agreements

84.   The BTP will continue to be funded by the railway industry. Certain operators will continue to be required to engage the police services of the BTP, while other operators will retain the choice. Section 33 provides for a system of Police Services Agreements ("PSAs"), that will act as the means by which the financial arrangements between the Authority and railway operators are calculated and set out. Section 34 gives the Secretary of State power to make orders requiring certain railway operators to enter into a PSA. Where an operator is required to enter into such an agreement but fails to do so, it will commit an offence if it then provides railway services, as defined in section 75(2).

85.   Section 35 makes provision on disputes relating to PSAs. Similar provision is currently contained in the Railways Act 1993, paragraph 6(b) of the British Transport Police Force Scheme 1963[4], and associated non-statutory rules. Disputes will be determined by the Secretary of State or a person nominated by him, with section 35(7) providing a means of appeal to the High Court from the Secretary of State's determination on a point of law.

Section 36-45: Police Regulations

86.   The Home Secretary has powers under the Police Act 1996 to make regulations regarding the government, administration and conditions of service in Home Office police forces.

87.   These regulations do not apply to the BTP. Instead the SRA, as employer of the force, applies similar provision to BTP constables through other means, notably conditions of employment and Force General Orders. Sections 36 (Police regulations: General), 37 (Police regulations: special constables), 38 (Police regulations: cadets) and 39 (British Transport Police Federation) enable the Authority to make regulations that are consistent with the equivalent regulations that apply to Home office police officers. Such BTP regulations may only differ from the regulations made under the Police Act 1996 to meet the specific needs of the Force.

---

[4] As set out in the Schedule to The British Transport Police Force Scheme 1963 (Amendment) Order 1994 (S.I. 1994/609)

88.　　Section 40 provides that the Authority can only make regulations if the Chief Constable and the staff associations have approved the draft.　Any such regulations would also need the prior approval of the Secretary of State.　This will ensure that the regulations proposed by the Authority do not differ unduly from regulations made under the Police Act 1996.

89.　　Section 42 enables the Secretary of State to make statutory regulations in relation to the BTP. This power would be used sparingly in circumstances where the Authority is unable to make regulations itself. These regulations would override any incompatible provisions of the regulations made by the Authority. The Secretary of State would be required to consult the Authority, the Chief Constable and BTP staff associations before making such regulations.

90.　　Sections 44 (equipment) and 45 (procedure and practice) enable the Secretary of State to make statutory regulations under powers in the Police Act 1996.　These regulations may extend to Scotland, even though the Police Act 1996 covers only England and Wales. This is to ensure that BTP equipment and procedures are harmonised across all the BTP's areas of operation.

Section 46: Conditions of service: Transport Police Conference

91.　　Section 46 specifies that where either the Secretary of State or the Authority are making regulations or taking a decision about the conditions of service of BTP constables, they must first refer the issue to the BTP "Conference". This is a forum consisting of an equal number of individuals nominated by the BTP Federation and the Authority to consider such issues and make recommendations that the Secretary of State or the Authority shall have regard to. An independent arbitrator can be appointed by either the Conference or the Secretary of State to make recommendations on behalf of the Conference if it is unable to agree.

Sections 47-49: Codes of Practice and service outside the BTP

92.　　The Police Act 1996 allows the Home Secretary to issue codes of practice for local police authorities and chief constables that relate to the discharge of their functions.　Sections 47 and 48 apply these Codes to the Authority and the BTP respectively, but also allow the Secretary of State to issue further codes to allow for the specific circumstances of the BTP.

93.　　Section 49 replicates provisions in the Police Act 1996.　BTP constables, like their Home Office counterparts, may temporarily serve with other police forces. This section allows the Secretary of State to make regulations to ensure that BTP officers on temporary service with another police force are not penalised on their return to the Force, i.e. they can retain promotion or service benefits obtained while on service outside the BTP.

Sections 50-55: Planning

94.　　Sections 50 (Policing objectives: Authority), 51 (Policing objectives: Secretary of

State), 52 (Railways policing plan), 53 (Performance targets) and 55 (Three-year strategy plan) are based on provisions of the Police Act 1996. Only where necessary to meet the specific needs of the Authority and the BTP do these provisions differ from the Police Act 1996. This is to ensure that the Authority operates in the same framework of governance as Home Office police authorities.

95.   Unlike police authorities established under the Police Acts 1996 and 1997, the BTP and its Committee are not subject to a "best value duty" under the Local Government Act 1999. However on a day-to-day basis, they act as if they were and apply the practices and principles of "best value" to the BTP. Section 54 (Performance directions) gives the Secretary of State the power to direct the Authority to apply any requirement that he could make in respect of a "best value authority" under the 1999 Act and so retain the current position regarding the BTP and "best value".

Sections 56-61: Information etc

96.   Sections 56 (Reports by Chief Constable), 57 (Annual report by Authority), 58 (Other reports to Secretary of State) and 59 (Statistics) are based on provisions of the Police Act 1996, regarding information that the Authority and Chief Constable are to provide to the Secretary of State, and in certain instances, lay before both Houses of Parliament or publish. Only where necessary to meet the specific needs of the Authority and the BTP have the corresponding provisions in the Police Act 1996 not been followed. Sections 60 and 61 (Inquiries) are based on provisions in the Police Act 1997 and allow the Secretary of State to set up an inquiry into any matter, most likely a major incident or serious crime, that was handled by the BTP.

Section 63-67: Inspection

97.   Her Majesty's Inspectors of Constabulary (as a body corporate known as HM Inspectorate of Constabulary - HMIC) inspect and report to the Secretary of State on the efficiency and effectiveness of all Home Office police forces under provisions in the Police Act 1996. These provisions also allow the Secretary of State to give certain directions to a Police Authority where HMIC consider that the whole or any part of the relevant police force is not efficient or effective, or will cease to be so unless remedial measures are taken. The BTP have not fallen under the statutory remit of HMIC in the past, but the BTP Committee has invited HMIC to undertake detailed assessments of the operational performance and organisation of the BTP every three years applying the same standards as for Home Office police forces.

98.   Section 63 (Inspection) places a statutory duty on HMIC to inspect and report to the Secretary of State on the BTP, both regularly and in response to a specific request. Sections 64 (Action after adverse inspection report), 65 (Remedial direction) and 66 (Action Plan) provide the Secretary of State with powers of direction following an adverse HMIC report on the BTP. These sections, modelled on similar provisions in the Police Act 1996, enable the Secretary of State to direct the Authority to take specified actions or ask it to produce an action plan to remedy any Force deficiencies. The procedures, including consulting with the Authority and Chief Constable, will apply to the Secretary of State regarding the BTP in the

same way as they apply to Home Office police forces.

99.   The main difference with Home Office police forces will be that the Authority will continue to meet the full costs of HMIC inspections of the BTP. This is in line with other non-Home Office police forces such as the Ministry of Defence Police Force, the UK Atomic Energy Authority Constabulary and the Isle of Man Police Force.   Inspections of Home Office police forces are funded centrally.

100.   The HMIC in England and Wales will continue to be responsible for inspections of the BTP as a whole.   Within Scotland, HMIC (Scotland) will be given a statutory duty to inspect the BTP and report to the Secretary of State in so far as the BTP operates in Scotland.

101.   Section 67 (Senior appointment: delegation of function) is also modelled on provisions in the Police Act 1996.   This provides the Secretary of State with a power to delegate his approval of the senior appointments in the BTP (under sections 21, 22 and 23) to HMIC.

Section 73: transitional and incidental provision

102.   Section 73 contains powers to make transitional provisions, including to a relevant pension scheme to ensure continuity following the establishment of the Authority. For example, subsection (3)(g) would enable modifications to be made to the procedural or structural arrangements of staff pension schemes (excluding benefit/contribution/funding structures) as a consequence of the new relationship between the Authority and Secretary of State.   Subsection (3)(f) would enable existing enactments about pension schemes to have immediate effect, e.g. to apply the provisions of Section 16 of the 1995 Pensions Act covering pension members' rights to select trustees.

Public sector financial and manpower cost

103.   The measures relating to the BTP will not require additional direct public expenditure, since the BTP will continue to be funded by the railway industry. The additional administrative cost of a police authority of 13 members over the cost of the current Committee of 9 is estimated at £50,000 per annum. This compares to the BTP's total annual budget of £136 million in 2003/04.

Human Rights assessment

104.   The BTP provisions of this Act are considered to be compatible with the Convention. Although BTP constables will be given the right to enter "private" property such as railways stations and rail vehicles, which engages the Article 8 right to a private life and the Article 1 of the First Protocol right to the peaceful enjoyment of possessions, it is considered that any such interference is justified.   The exercise of this power is limited to defined pieces of railways property, and is available to BTP constables so that they may ensure public safety, and prevent crime and disorder.

105.   Certain persons, such as train companies, will be required by order made under

provisions in this Act to enter in to PSAs with the new Authority, and under these agreements payment must be made to the Authority. This engages Article 1 of the First Protocol, which protects the economic interests of a person running a business. It is considered that any interference this obligation causes with this right can be justified on the basis that it is in the general interest that the railways are policed, and that if the Authority were not funded then it could not make provision for a police force for the railways.

Part 4 - Shipping: Alcohol and Drugs

106. This Part extends to any professional and (subject to any exceptions made by regulations) to any non-professional mariner sailing in United Kingdom waters, as well as to mariners in United Kingdom-registered ships elsewhere.

Background

107. Prior to this Act there was no specific legislation to regulate alcohol consumption in the maritime industry apart from a general provision in section 58 of the Merchant Shipping Act 1995. That section made it an offence for the master or a seaman employed in a UK-registered ship, or in a foreign ship in a UK port or in UK waters on its way to or from a UK port, to endanger his ship or other ships by reason of being under the influence of drink (or drugs). There is no maximum blood/alcohol limit specified.

108. Following the Marine Accident Investigation Branch's (MAIB) inquiry into the Marchioness disaster in 1989, the then Government asked John Hayes to conduct a wider inquiry into river safety. The Hayes Report, published in 1992, included a recommendation that a breath test should be introduced, similar to that applying to motor vehicle drivers which would apply to the skippers and crew of all vessels. Subsequently, in August 1999 the Government announced an inquiry to review all the arrangements to ensure safety on the Thames. The inquiry chairman, Lord Justice Clarke, made a number of recommendations, in particular that primary legislation should be used to introduce alcohol legislation for vessels on similar lines to that existing in relation to road traffic. These recommendations were further reinforced by Lord Justice Clarke in his report of the Formal Investigation into the collision between the Marchioness and the Bowbelle.

Commentary on sections

109. Part 4 of this Act provides for the creation of statutory alcohol limits for mariners, and the creation of alcohol and drug-testing regimes. These provisions largely mirror provisions for road users and safety-critical staff on railways and related transport systems.

110. This Act puts in place an alcohol-testing regime in a similar manner to that already existing in other transport modes. The provisions in this Act therefore largely mirror those of the Road Traffic Act 1988, the Road Traffic Offenders Act 1988 and the Transport and Works Act 1992. The Act also introduces a drug-testing regime into this Part, which reflects the regime introduced in relation to road traffic by virtue of section 107 and Schedule 7 of this Act. The following table shows the sections of the current Act which are drawn from provisions in the 1988 Acts and 1992 Act, along with a brief description of their effects.

RTS Section	Road Traffic Act 1988	Road Traffic Offenders Act 1988	Transport & Works Act 1992	Description
78(2) 79(2) and 80(2)	Section 4		Section 27(1)	Being impaired through drugs or alcohol
78(3) 79(3) and 80(3)	Section 5		Section 27(2)	Having alcohol in body above prescribed limit
81	Section 11(2)		Section 38(2)	Prescribed limit
83	See table on face of Act	See table on face of Act	Sections 29, 31, 32, 33, 34, 35	See table on face of Act
85	Sections 4(6) and 6(5) & (6)		Section 30	Powers of arrest without a warrant
86	Section 6(6)		Section 30(3) and 30(4)	Right of entry

Section 78: Professional staff on duty

111.   If a fisherman is charged with an offence under section 78(2) or 78(3), section 78(5) makes it a defence for him to show that he took the drug for medicinal purposes, in accordance with medical advice or where he had no reason to expect it would affect him adversely. The equivalent provision was contained in section 117(2) of the Merchant Shipping Act 1995, which section is now repealed.

Section 79: Professional staff off duty

112.   Section 79 includes off duty professional seamen who may be called on in an emergency at any time to protect the safety of passengers. Section 79(5) extends to this class of professional staff the defence of having taken a drug for medicinal purposes.

Section 80: Non-professionals

113.   Section 80 applies to non-professionals (recreational mariners). The offence created is a "moving" offence, which only applies if the vessel is in motion (in contrast to sections 78 and 79) and the offence does not apply to passengers. Section 80 also provides a power to except, by regulations, non-professional mariners who do not pose substantial safety risks from the prescribed limits and the requirement to provide specimens.

Section 83: Specimens, &c.

114.   Section 83 replicates certain provisions of the Road Traffic Act 1988, amended where appropriate to apply to shipping, adopting in relation to mariners the same procedures for taking specimens as are applicable to motorists. This section also replicates, as similarly

amended, the new provisions of the Road Traffic Act 1988 introduced by section 107 and set out in Schedule 7 to this Act in relation to preliminary impairment tests and preliminary drug tests.

115.   Section 83 also applies certain provisions of the Road Traffic Offenders Act 1988, to offences under sections 78, 79 or 80 of this Act by substituting navigation functions for references in the 1988 Act to driving a motor car.

Section 84: Detention pending arrival of police

116.   Prior to this Act, local bye-laws allowed some harbour authority officials to exercise powers to detain ships whose pilots were suspected to be committing an offence of being impaired by drink or drugs. Section 84 extends this regime to allow marine officials to detain a vessel when they reasonably suspect that a person on board is committing an offence under this Part. However, in order not to affect the operational effectiveness of the armed forces, this section does not apply to ships which are being used for a purpose of Her Majesty's forces or which form part of the Royal Fleet Auxiliary.

Section 86: Right of entry

117.   A constable in uniform may use reasonable force to board a ship or enter any other place if he reasonably suspects that he may wish to exercise a power under this Act, e.g. to administer a preliminary breath test. In exercising his right of entry he may be accompanied. This section does not extend to Scotland where adequate common law powers of entry already exist.

Section 88: Orders and regulations

118.   Section 88 makes provision for the making of various orders and regulations under this Part.   Under section 80 regulations may be made to create exceptions removing non-professional mariners in certain specified categories from the offence of exceeding the prescribed alcohol limit.   Regulations may be made under section 81 altering the prescribed alcohol limits.   Regulations may be made under section 83 to amend the table, for example, to reflect any future changes in road traffic legislation.   Finally, orders can be made under section 84 to designate marine officials who are able to detain a ship.

Section 90: Crown application &c.

119.   Section 90(1) and (4) excepts members of Her Majesty's forces and members of visiting forces (including civilians attached to such visiting forces) from the offences created by this Part when they are acting in the course of their duties. This is because in such circumstances they would be subject, as the case may be, either to UK service law or, in the case of a visiting force from another country, to the service laws of that country. Otherwise, under section 90(2) this Part applies to any civilian person who is in the service of the Crown. Section 90(3) prevents marine officials from detaining any ship which is being used by Her Majesty's forces or a ship forming part of the Royal Fleet Auxiliary Service.

Section 91: Territorial application

120.   Section 91(2) and (3) ensures that the Scottish common law powers of entry for obtaining evidence are maintained in the case of mariners, as is currently the case for car drivers, train drivers and now aviation personnel who may have committed an alcohol or drug related offence. It disapplies provisions contained in this Act giving the police rights of entry, since these would risk conflicting with the common law powers available in Scotland.

Public sector financial and manpower cost

121.   It is difficult to quantify the financial costs to the public purse from the introduction and enforcement of an alcohol limit, as well as preliminary impairment and drug-testing, for mariners. Use will be made of current resources such as harbour launches and search and rescue helicopters to assist the police to reach a ship in order to conduct preliminary alcohol and drug tests or the preliminary impairment test. Training to cover techniques in boarding ships at sea by means of helicopter or ship to ship transfers will be provided by the Maritime and Coastguard Agency. In terms of testing apparatus, there would be minimal costs for implementation of the alcohol provisions, since the testing regime would use equipment already in use for alcohol testing on the roads, or which will be brought into use for drug testing. The number of tests required is expected to be low, as would be the number of prosecution cases.

122.   Alcohol and drugs provisions in the marine sector will not require recruitment of more public sector workers, though there will be additional responsibilities on existing police, marine or legal officers.

Human Rights assessment

123.   This Part potentially engages Article 5 (right to liberty and security), Article 6 (right to a fair trial) and Article 8 (right to respect for private and family life) of the European Convention on Human Rights. Article 5 is subject to the qualification of lawful arrest on reasonable suspicion that an offence has been committed or for its prevention. The powers of arrest and detention contained in this Part are considered necessary and proportionate and within the qualification mentioned.

124.   Article 6 (which is linked to a privilege against self-incrimination) is engaged principally by the provisions requiring specimens of breath, blood or urine to be provided by a suspect. However, the courts have held that the privilege is not absolute in circumstances where a proportionate response is required to combat a serious social problem. This is considered to be such a case.

125.   Article 8 is subject to the qualification that a public authority may interfere with the right to private and family life provided that it does so in a proportionate manner for the prevention of crime and protection of the public.

126.   This Part is considered to be compatible with Convention rights.

Part 5 - Aviation: Alcohol and Drugs

127.   This Part extends to the flight and cabin crew of an aircraft, air traffic controllers and licensed aircraft maintenance engineers in the United Kingdom. It also applies to the crew of an aircraft registered in the United Kingdom wherever it may be in the world.

Background

128.   At present the only specific legislation to regulate alcohol consumption in the aviation industry is in the Air Navigation Order 2000 ("the ANO") [5], made under the Civil Aviation Act 1982.

129.   The ANO makes it an offence for a crew member of an aircraft, an air traffic controller or a licensed maintenance engineer to be under the influence of drink or drugs so as to impair his capacity to carry out his aviation related functions. (See articles 13(8), 65(2) and 96.)

130.   Previously, there was no set limit as to the amount of alcohol that could be consumed prior to carrying out an aviation function, although it was an offence for a member of the flight deck crew, an air traffic controller or a licensed maintenance engineer to carry out their licence privileges whilst impaired through drink or drugs. Similarly, there was previously no power to test a relevant individual suspected of being under the influence of alcohol or drugs.

Commentary on sections

131.   This Act puts in place an alcohol-testing regime in a similar manner to that already existing in other transport modes. The provisions in this Act therefore largely mirror those of the Road Traffic Act 1988, the Road Traffic Offenders Act 1988 and the Transport and Works Act 1992. The following table shows the sections of the current Act which are drawn from provisions in the 1988 Acts and 1992 Act, along with a brief description of their effects.

RTS Section	Road Traffic Act 1988	Road Traffic Offenders Act 1988	Transport & Works Act 1992	Description
92	Sections 4(1) and (5)		Sections 27(1) and (4)	Being impaired through drugs or alcohol
93	Section 5(1)(a)		Section 27(2)	Having alcohol in body above prescribed limit
93(2) & (3)	Section 11(2)		Section 38(2)	Prescribed limit
96	See table on face of Act	See table on face of Act	Sections 29, 31, 32, 33, 34, 35	See table on face of Act

_____

[5] S.I. 2000/1562

RTS Section	Road Traffic Act 1988	Road Traffic Offenders Act 1988	Transport & Works Act 1992	Description
97	Sections 4(6) and 6(5)		Sections 30(1) and (2)	Powers of arrest without a warrant
98	Sections 4(7) and 6(6)		Section 30(3) and 30(4)	Right of entry

Section 92: Being unfit for duty

132.   Section 92 makes it an offence to perform an aviation function or an ancillary activity whilst impaired through alcohol or drugs.

Section 93: Prescribed limit

133.   Section 93(1) makes it an offence to perform or prepare to perform certain aviation-related functions with more than a prescribed level of alcohol in the body. Subsections (2) and (3) set the prescribed blood/alcohol alcohol limits at 20 milligrammes of alcohol per 100 millilitres of blood for those activities carried out by aircrew and air traffic controllers, and 80 milligrams per 100 millilitres for licensed aircraft maintenance engineers. In the former case, this is a quarter of the limit prescribed by the Road Traffic Act 1988 and the Transport and Works Act 1992 for drivers and railway workers respectively. The different limits reflect the fact that although licensed aircraft maintenance engineers perform a safety critical role in aviation, they do not necessarily require the same speed of reaction as aircrew or air traffic controllers may need in an emergency situation. The equivalent limits in respect of breath and of urine are also set out in this section.

Section 94: Aviation functions

134.   Section 94 subsections (3), (4), (5) and (6) apply the offences of being either over the limit or unfit, to people preparing to carry out an aviation function or otherwise holding themselves ready to carry out one of those functions by virtue of being on duty or standby.

Section 95: Penalty

135.   The penalties set out in section 95 are set at the same level as those currently applying to aircrew and air traffic controllers under Article 122 of the ANO. This section will bring the penalty for licensed maintenance engineers under the influence of alcohol or drugs into line with them.

Section 96: Specimens, &c.

136.   Section 96 replicates certain provisions of the Road Traffic Act 1988 and the Road Traffic Offenders Act 1988, amended where appropriate to apply to aviation. Section 96 also replicates the new provisions of the Road Traffic Act 1988, set out in Schedule 7 to this Act, amended where appropriate to apply to aviation.

Sections 97 and 98: Arrest without a warrant, Right of entry

137.   Section 97 provides the police with the power to arrest suspected offenders. Section 98 provides the police with powers to board an aircraft or enter any place in connection with an offence committed under sections 92 and 93. It spells out that the police may use reasonable force in exercising these powers and that they may be accompanied when doing so.

Sections 100 and 101: Crown and military application

138.   Sections 100 and 101 apply the offences created to personnel in organisations such as the police and customs, but not to service personnel operating in the course of their military duties. When acting in the course of their duties, service personnel may be subject to separate disciplinary procedures if found under the influence of alcohol or drugs. However, service men and women carrying out aviation functions during their free time will be subject to this legislation.

139.   Section 101 disapplies the offences for the civil or military components of visiting military forces and for personnel belonging to international headquarters or defence organisations such as NATO, but only whilst carrying out their duties. UK military personnel in analogous circumstances are protected similarly from criminal prosecution when they are based overseas.

140.   Section 101 relies upon certain definitions in the Army Act 1955, the Visiting Forces Act 1952 and the International Headquarters and Defence Organisations Act 1964. These are as follows:

- Section 225(1) of the Army Act 1955 provides that:

   "Her Majesty's air forces, Her Majesty's military forces or Her Majesty's naval forces, except where otherwise expressly provided, does not include any Commonwealth force"

- Section 3 of the Visiting Forces Act 1952 protects members of visiting forces and members of the civilian components of such forces from being tried for an offence by a United Kingdom Court in certain circumstances.

- By virtue of section 12(1) of the Visiting Forces Act 1952, "visiting force" for the purpose of section 3 means:

   "any body, contingent or detachment of the forces of a country to which [the] provision applies, being a body, contingent or detachment for the time being present in the United Kingdom on the invitation of Her Majesty's Government in the United Kingdom".

- The International Headquarters and Defence Organisations Act 1964 defines headquarters as a headquarters or organisation designated by Order in Council under that Act. The International Headquarters and Defence Organisations (Designation and Privileges) Order 1965 lists the organisations to which the Act applies, for example Allied Forces North Western Europe. A military member of a headquarters is defined by the 1964 Act as:

   "a member of any country's forces who is for the time being appointed to serve in the United Kingdom under the orders of a headquarters, except that it does not include a member of the home forces."

- Section 10 of the Visiting Forces Act 1952 and paragraph 2 of the Schedule to the International Headquarters and Defence Organisations Act 1964 make similar provision to define a member of the civilian component of a visiting force and a civilian member of a headquarters etc. Such a member must satisfy certain conditions relating to his passport which should be issued by a foreign government, contain an entry confirming his status and a note that the Secretary of State recognises that entry.

Section 102: Territorial application

141. Part 5 applies to functions or activities in the United Kingdom and to "flight functions" or "flight activities" abroad carried out on UK registered aircraft. There is power by Order in Council to extend the provisions to the Channel Isles or to a British Overseas Territory.

142. Section 102(4) and (5) ensure that the Scottish common law powers of entry apply to the investigation of offences committed under the aviation part of this Act in the same way that they apply to alcohol and drug offences committed on Scottish roads, railways and, under part 4 of this Act, to shipping. Section 102(4) provides that section 98 does not extend to Scotland. Section 102(5) expressly preserves the rights of entry which police in Scotland already have.

Public sector financial and manpower cost

143. It is difficult to quantify the financial costs to the public purse from the introduction and enforcement of an alcohol limit for aviation. The same issues on police resources apply as for mariners. The lower blood/alcohol limit for aircraft crew and air traffic controllers will mean that existing police roadside screening devices will need to be re-assessed and approved for use at the new aviation limit. It is anticipated that the cost of the necessary work to support the re-certification of the six most commonly used models of screening device currently used by UK police forces will be in the region of £30,000. A limited number of new screening devices would need to be purchased by those police forces exclusively using older screening equipment not suitable for use at the aviation limit. Each new device costs in the region of £450, but the number of new devices required would depend on the extent of aviation activity in the police area, and the cost offset by their potential ability to be used in normal road traffic cases. It is not possible to quantify the number of tests that may be carried out, but it is anticipated that approximately 10 to 15 cases per year may be brought before the courts. The Department for Constitutional Affairs has indicated that the associated policy costs to the courts as a result of these additional prosecutions, could be absorbed within its existing resources.

144. Alcohol and drugs provisions, both in the marine and aviation sectors, will not require recruitment of more public sector workers, though there will be additional responsibilities on existing police, marine and legal officers.

Human Rights assessment

145. This Part potentially engages Article 5 (right to liberty and security), Article 6 (right

to a fair trial) and Article 8 (right to respect for private and family life) of the European Convention on Human Rights.

146.   Article 5 is subject to the qualification of lawful arrest on reasonable suspicion that an offence has been committed or for its prevention.   The powers of arrest and detention contained in this Part are considered necessary and proportionate and within the qualification mentioned.

147.   Article 6 (which is linked to the privilege against self-incrimination) is engaged principally by the provisions requiring specimens of breath, blood or urine to be provided by a suspect.   However, the courts have held that the privilege is not absolute in circumstances where a proportionate response is required to combat a serious social problem. This is considered to be such a case.

148.   Article 8 is subject to the qualification that a public authority may interfere with the right to private and family life provided that it does so in a proportionate manner for the prevention of crime and protection of the public.

149.   This Part is considered to be compatible with the Convention.

Part 6 – Miscellaneous

Section 103: International Carriage by Rail

150.   This part extends throughout the United Kingdom

Background

151.   The United Kingdom is a signatory to the Protocol of Vilnius 1999 ("the Protocol") which modifies the Convention concerning International Carriage by Rail ("COTIF[6]") 1980, by presenting a new Convention text[7]. The Protocol of Vilnius will need to be ratified by the UK, but before that can happen the UK must have the necessary legislation in place to be able to give effect to the new COTIF when it comes in to force. This Act makes the necessary provision to allow for this. Like the existing 1980 COTIF[8], the new COTIF provides a uniform system of laws, which will apply to the carriage of passengers, luggage and freight in international through traffic by rail, in order to facilitate the development of that traffic. There are currently 41 signatories to the 1980 COTIF. Uniform systems of law have been in operation for many years: the first international convention concerning the carriage of goods was signed in 1893.

152.   Under the 1980 COTIF there are several sets of rules, known as "Uniform Rules" which make provision on:

---

[6] An acronym for "Convention Relative aux Transports Internationaux Ferroviaires".
[7] Miscellaneous No.21 (2000), Command Paper 4873,
[8] Consolidated text published in Treaty Series No.73 (1997), Command Paper 3812.

- contracts for the international carriage of passengers (known as the CIV Uniform Rules)

- contracts for the international carriage of goods (freight) (known as the CIM Uniform Rules) with annexes dealing with, amongst other things, the carriage of dangerous goods (known as the RID Regulation)

153.   COTIF 1980 is being modified primarily to reflect major changes in railway management and operations particularly following EC Directive 91/440/EEC (29 July 1991) on the development of the Community's railways.

154.   In particular, the changes to the COTIF 1980 reflect the following developments in EC Member States:

- increasing separation of infrastructure management from train operators; and

- introduction of open access rights, opening up the possibility of more than one operator on any one network.

155.   The CIV Uniform Rules also ensure that minimum levels of compensation exist for certain incidents throughout all signatory states. These levels have been increased in the new COTIF, which will be of benefit to international rail users generally.

156.   The Protocol of Vilnius signed on 3 June 1999:

- provides brand new CIV Uniform Rules (Appendix A) and CIM Uniform Rules (Appendix B);

- makes RID a free standing Appendix, (Appendix C)

and recognising the importance of these issues for facilitating international traffic introduces new Uniform Rules for:

- Contracts of use of vehicles in international rail traffic (CUV) (Appendix D)

- Contracts of use of infrastructure in international rail traffic (CUI) (Appendix E)

- The validation of technical standards and prescriptions applicable to railway material intended to be used in international traffic (APTU) (Appendix F)

- The technical admission of railway material used in international traffic (ATMF) (Appendix G)

157.   Article 6§8 and §9 of the Protocol makes transitional provision for contracts entered into under COTIF 1980.

158.   The Protocol and the new COTIF it presents was presented to Parliament as a Command Paper CM 4873 in October 2000.

159.   The new COTIF will come into force three months after the Protocol is ratified by

two-thirds of signatories to the Convention. This is unlikely to be before 2004.

160.   Although the UK will ratify the Protocol by means of the Royal Prerogative, once the new COTIF comes in to force as a matter of international law it will not have the force of law in UK until the relevant provisions of this Act are brought into force and the corresponding domestic regulations are made. The International Transport Conventions Act 1983, which currently gives effect to the COTIF 1980 is not sufficiently flexible to deal with the new COTIF. The sections in this Act, combined with the domestic implementing regulations are designed to provide the necessary flexibility to give effect to the new COTIF. Redundant provisions of the 1983 Act will be repealed by the new regulations.

161.   The new COTIF covers certain matters that are already covered by EC law. In particular, the new APTU and ATMF appendices address the same matters as the EC Directives on the interoperability of the European rail network (Directives 96/48/EC & 2001/16/EC). The new COTIF does however recognise that, for EC Member States, EC law shall prevail.

Commentary on section

162.   Section 103 provides the Secretary of State with the power to make regulations to give effect to the new COTIF in the UK. Such regulations must be approved by both Houses of Parliament.

Schedule 6 – Convention on International Carriage by Rail

163.   Paragraph 1 defines the word "regulations" in Schedule 6 as meaning regulations made in connection with COTIF either under section 103(1) or section 2 of the European Communities Act 1972.

164.   Paragraphs 2, 3, 4, and 5 list the provisions which may be included in regulations. The powers may only be exercised for the purposes of giving effect to the new COTIF. They include, but are not limited to, the power to:

- give effect to the new COTIF in UK law,

- change UK law for the purposes of giving effect to the new COTIF,

- make provision for certain future changes to the new COTIF automatically to form part of UK law; and

- impose conditions before any person may exercise a right or do something to which the Convention applies.

165.   In particular paragraph 3 will enable regulations to provide that most changes to the new COTIF which take place in future will flow through directly into UK law. This is intended to cater for the provisions in the new COTIF which allow certain technical changes to the terms of the Convention to be made by a Committee process and automatically to come into effect: an example might be the adoption of a new uniform technical prescription under

the APTU appendix to the new Convention. Although the Government proposes that most modifications to the new COTIF and its appendices will flow through in to UK law, the Government's intention is that modifications made by the General Assembly (which is composed of the new COTIF's signatory states) should require specific approval by Parliament. This is because such modifications could potentially be of greater impact in the UK.

166.   Paragraph 6 enables the creation of sanctions (including criminal sanctions) for the purposes of ensuring that a duty under the new COTIF may be enforced.

167.   Since the new COTIF covers damages and compensation arising from the international carriage of passengers and freight, paragraph 7 would allow regulations to make provision to prevent double recovery. Provision could also be made to allow a UK court to take account of actual or potential legal proceedings outside the UK, when taking decisions during UK proceedings.

168.   Paragraph 8 enables regulations to be made which deal with the enforcement of judgements, which may in particular deal with the enforcement of foreign judgements.

169.   Paragraph 9 provides that the regulations may make provision for the "Special Drawing Right" (the new COTIF's international currency unit) to be converted into sterling.

Public sector financial and manpower cost

170.   It is not expected that implementation of COTIF into UK law will require any significant additional public expenditure, nor that there will be an additional public manpower burden.

Human Rights assessment

171.   The COTIF provisions of this Act are considered to be compatible with the ECHR. One particular effect of the COTIF provisions of this Act, and the regulations which may be made under those provisions, will be to ensure that certain dangerous goods may not be carried by rail. It is considered that where this interferes with a person's economic interests in running a business (protected by Article 1 of the First Protocol), this prohibition may be justified on general public interest grounds. The prohibition also goes towards ensuring that the UK upholds the Article 8 right to respect for a person's home which right could otherwise be affected by environmental blight or pollution from the carriage of those goods.

Section 104: Office of Rail Regulation: general duties

172.   Section 104 makes a minor amendment to Section 4(5) of the Railways Act 1993 by repealing the words shown in bold:

> "The Office of Rail Regulation shall also be under a duty in exercising the functions assigned or transferred to it under this Part;
> > (a) to have regard to the financial position of the [Strategic Rail] Authority in discharging its functions **under this Part**."

This ensures that the Office has regard to the Strategic Rail Authority's financial position in respect of all of its functions. It is a consequential amendment not picked up in the Transport Act 2000 arising from the creation of the Strategic Rail Authority in place of the Franchising Director. The Authority's financial position, unlike that of the Franchising Director, is not limited to discharging its functions under the Part of the 1993 Act referred to in the deleted words.

Section 105: Railway safety levy

173.   Section 105 extends to England, Scotland and Wales.

Background

174.   Under the Health and Safety at Work etc Act 1974, the Health and Safety Executive (HSE) is responsible for a range of regulatory work including inspection activities applied to the rail industry. Since October 1999, there has been a charge for this work, on an hourly basis. Such charges only cover part of the cost of HSE's work on railway safety; for example they do not cover work relating to policy-making or all operational activities.

175.   Ministers agreed that the impact of charging would be reviewed after two years. The review revealed that the existing charging regime was seen as bureaucratic, and stakeholders could not easily budget for charges. HSE held a consultation exercise with industry stakeholders on the principle of a railway safety levy between the end of November and 20 December 2002.

176.   Regulations to require the payment of a levy require primary legislation, because levies cannot be imposed under Regulations made under section 43(2) of the Health and Safety at Work etc Act 1974 (which provides vires for the existing charging regime).

Commentary on section

177.   Section 105(1) inserts a new section 43A in the Health and Safety at Work etc Act 1974, giving the Secretary of State power to make regulations introducing a compulsory railway safety levy on the railway industry. The Health and Safety Commission will be able to propose such regulations to the Secretary of State after consultation.

178.   Section 105(2) amends section 28(1)(a) of the Health and Safety at Work etc Act 1974 so that information provided under the proposed regulations will be subject to the provisions of that section.

Public sector financial and manpower cost

179.   As the purpose of a rail safety levy would be to fund the existing and planned railway safety activities of HSE in a different way, it is not considered that there will be any additional public sector financial or manpower costs.

Human Rights assessment

180. This section potentially engages Article 1 (right to the peaceful enjoyment of possessions) of the European Convention on Human Rights. The right under Article 1 is qualified by Article 1(2), which says that:

> "this shall not in any way impair the right of a state to enforce such laws as it deems necessary to control the use of property in accordance with the general interest, or to secure the payment of taxes or other contributions or penalties."

181. The Government considers that the provisions of new section 43A are compatible with the Convention.

Section 106: Railway security services

182. This section extends to England, Wales and Scotland. It amends the Railways Act 1993 by adding a new section 121A.

Background

183. The Secretary of State for Transport has the power to serve instructions (under the Railways Act 1993) on owners and operators of relevant railway assets (networks, stations, light maintenance depots, track or rolling stock) and anyone who provides a railway service. These would detail the security provisions they must implement to protect the travelling public, staff and infrastructure.

184. Revised instructions covering the security of stations are currently being drafted, and are expected to be served on the industry in the summer of 2003. Further instructions covering other aspects of the rail network will be issued through 2003 and 2004. These instructions will give legal force to current security requirements contained in the National Railways Security Programme.

185. It is expected that the instructions will include requirements for the searching of stations, trains and other facilities and screening of baggage at left-luggage facilities.

186. Where the person who is required to comply with the instruction chooses to contract out such security work, the new section will allow the Secretary of State to ensure that only persons approved by him can carry out the work (or train others to carry it out).

187. A similar section in the Anti-Terrorism, Crime and Security Act 2001, gave the Secretary of State the same listing powers with regard to security providers to the aviation industry. Under the Channel Tunnel Act 1987, similar powers are already available covering the Channel Tunnel industries. The new section will ensure that the Railway industry is consistent with these.

Commentary on section

188. This section only creates an enabling power. Regulations will have to be drafted,

made and laid before the Parliament before listing can have statutory effect.

Public sector financial and manpower cost

189.   The railway security measures will probably require slight additional public expenditure over and above that already required to administer the listing of aviation security providers, but this is unlikely to amount to more than a few days of staff time in processing applications.

Human Rights assessment

190.   The amendment to the Railways Act 1993 does not appear to involve any conflicts with the Human Rights Act 1998. Article 6 (right to fair trial) of the European Convention on Human Rights is potentially engaged, but there must be provision in the regulations for an appeal if a person ceases to be approved and is withdrawn from the list. Similarly Article 7 (no punishment without law) is potentially relevant, but any criminal offences created by the new regulations will not operate retrospectively, so it is considered that this section is compatible with the Convention.

Section 107 & Schedule 7 – Road traffic: testing for drink and drugs

191.   Schedule 7 contains six new sections designed to replace section 6 of the Road Traffic Act 1988 (breath tests) with new powers for the police to administer three preliminary tests – a breathalyser test, a test indicating whether a person is unfit to drive due to drink or drugs and a test for the presence of drugs in a person's body. Schedule 7 also makes consequential amendments.

192.   The new section 6 enables a constable to require a person to co-operate with any one or more preliminary tests in certain circumstances. The person would commit an offence if without reasonable excuse he failed to co-operate. The circumstances include –

a) where a constable reasonably suspects that the person –

- has been driving, attempting to drive or in charge of a motor vehicle on a road or other public place while having alcohol or a drug in his body or while unfit to drive because of a drug and still has alcohol or a drug in his body or is still under the influence of a drug;
- has committed a traffic offence while the vehicle was in motion,

b) where an accident occurs owing to the presence of a motor vehicle on a road or other public place.

193.   The preliminary tests are:

- a breath test whereby a specimen of breath is taken by means of a device approved by the Secretary of State which indicates whether the proportion of alcohol in a person's breath or blood is likely to exceed the prescribed limit (section 6A).

- an impairment test which consists of a series of physical tasks set by the constable. By observing the person's ability to perform these tasks, and making such other observations of the person's physical state as the constable thinks expedient, the constable can obtain an indication whether the person is unfit to drive and, if he is, whether his unfitness is likely to be due to drink or drugs. The Secretary of State is required to issue and to keep under review a code of practice regarding such tests (section 6B).

- a drug test whereby a specimen of sweat or saliva is used, by means of a device approved by the Secretary of State, for the purpose of obtaining an indication whether a person has a drug in his body (section 6C).

194.   Sections 6A, 6B and 6C also make provision as to where a test may be carried out.

195.   Sections 6D and 6E make provision about powers of arrest and powers of entry respectively in connection with the administration of the preliminary tests.

Section 108: Traffic regulation on long-distance routes

196.   An order made under section 108 extends to England. The section gives the Secretary of State power to make an order restricting vehicular traffic on long-distance routes designated under the National Parks and Access to the Countryside Act 1949.

Section 109: Road traffic: fixed penalty

197.   Section 109 is a drafting amendment to correct an error to ensure that section 76(2) of the Road Traffic Offenders Act 1988 makes sense. It now reads:

> "No proceedings shall be brought against any person for the offence to which the conditional offer relates until—
>
>   a) in England and Wales, the person by or on whose behalf the conditional offer was sent receives notice in accordance with subsection (4) or (5) below"

Section 110: Seat belts: delivery drivers

198.   Section 110 replaces the current provisions of section 14(2)(b)(i) of the Road Traffic Act 1988. Section 14 is an enabling power under which the Secretary of State may make regulations requiring persons to wear seat belts when driving or riding in motor vehicles. Subsection (2)(b) provides that any such regulations must include the specified exceptions.

199.   The revised exception would apply to goods vehicle drivers and passengers when undertaking deliveries or collections. It would be based on the prescribed distance that may be travelled without a seat belt. At present the exception is available to those vehicle users "engaged in making local rounds of deliveries or collections" without prescribing clear criteria for establishing when a person is so engaged.

Section 111: Highways: snow and ice

200. This section extends to England and Wales. Section 111 provides a duty on a highway authority to ensure, so far as is reasonably practicable, that safe passage along a highway is not endangered by snow and ice.

Background

201. On 15 June 2000, in the case of *Goodes v East Sussex County Council*[9], the House of Lords decided that the duty of a highway authority, under section 41 of the Highways Act 1980, to maintain a highway did not include a duty to keep the highway safe by preventing ice from forming. They considered that if such a duty were desirable, that would be a matter for Parliament.

202. The duty provided by this section is similar to one already existing in Scotland, contained in section 34 of the Roads (Scotland) Act 1984.

Section 112: Shipping legislation: application to structures, craft &c.

203. This section extends throughout the United Kingdom.

204. Section 112 provides a new, extended power for the Secretary of State to make an order so that any shipping provision may be applied, disapplied or modified in relation to things used on water.

205. A "shipping provision" is defined so that it could include a provision made in this Act (when enacted) or in the Merchant Shipping Act 1995, or in subordinate legislation made under either Act, or a provision made in or under another Act. To be a shipping provision it must also expressly apply in relation to ships, vessels or boats.

206. The order may provide for other legislation to take precedence, for example where there are relevant harbour byelaws in place.

207. The Secretary of State may use the power in order to apply the provisions of the Act relating to alcohol testing of mariners to users of personal watercraft (such as jetskis[TM]), or to those in charge of chain ferries. Current case law casts doubt on whether these things would otherwise be "ships" for the purposes of Part 4 of the Act.

208. An order could also be made in order to apply the UK's merchant shipping regulations relating to the prevention of collisions to personal watercraft, even if they are not being used "at sea". Regulations relating to the survey of ships could be made to apply to chain ferries by means of such an order.

209. An order could be used to clarify the application of other legislation. For example, various Acts relating to public health and regulation of activities near the seashore confer

---

[9] [2000] 3 All ER 603

byelaw-making powers on local authorities with regard to vessels used for pleasure purposes or pleasure boats. These powers (e.g. under section 76 of the Public Health Act 1961 and section 231 of the Public Health Act 1936) are currently used occasionally to prosecute users of personal watercraft for breaches of byelaws. However, if it were considered necessary to create an order under the Merchant Shipping Act 1995 in relation to personal watercraft, this order might cast doubt on the application of these other Acts to such craft. An order under section 112 of this Act might therefore be necessary to clarify the application of other Acts.

Section 113: Maritime security services

210.   This section extends to the whole of the United Kingdom. It amends the Aviation and Maritime Security Act 1990 by adding a new section 36A.

Background

211.   The Secretary of State for Transport has the power to serve directions (under the Aviation & Maritime Security Act 1990) on various classes of people operating in the maritime industry, detailing the security provisions which they must implement to protect the travelling public, staff and infrastructure from unlawful acts of violence.

212.   Directions served on operators include such requirements as the screening of passengers, staff, visitors, luggage and ships' stores.

213.   Where the directed person chooses to contract out such security work, section 107 will allow the Secretary of State to ensure that only companies listed by him can carry out the work (or train others to carry it out).

214.   A similar section in the Anti-Terrorism, Crime and Security Act 2001, gave the Secretary of State the same listing powers with regard to security providers to the aviation industry. Under the Channel Tunnel Act 1987, similar powers are already available covering the Channel Tunnel industries. The new section will ensure that the maritime industry is consistent with these.

Commentary on section

215.   This section only creates an enabling power. Regulations will have to be drafted, made and laid before Parliament before listing can have statutory effect.

Public sector financial and manpower cost

216.   The maritime security measures will probably require slight additional public expenditure over and above that already required to administer the aviation security providers listing, but this is unlikely to amount to more than a few days of staff time in processing applications.

Human Rights assessment

217.   This amendment to the Aviation and Maritime Security Act 1990 does not appear to involve any conflicts with the Human Rights Act 1998. Article 6 (right to fair trial) of the European Convention on Human Rights is potentially engaged, but there must be provision in the regulations for an appeal if a person ceases to be approved and is withdrawn from the list. Similarly Article 7 (no punishment without law) is potentially relevant, but any criminal offences created by the new regulations will not operate retrospectively, so it is considered that this section is compatible with the Convention.

Sections 114 and 115: Railways in London: transfers & information

218.   These sections extend to England, Wales and Scotland.

Background

219.   The Greater London Authority Act 1999 (GLA Act) envisaged the transfer of London Underground (LUL) from London Regional Transport (LRT) to Transport for London (TfL) after the Public Private Partnership agreements for the London Underground had come into effect. This Act provides a mechanism to allow contracts to operate as intended on transfer from London Regional Transport to Transport for London, and on any subsequent transfer between Transport for London's subsidiaries.

220.   The Greater London Authority Act 1999 did not contemplate the possibility of a significant delay between completion of a Public Private Partnership agreement and transfer of the London Underground to Transport for London. This Act therefore also allows for certain provisions in the GLA Act relating to public private partnership agreements for the London Underground and the special insolvency provisions to come into effect before the transfer of the London Underground to Transport for London.

Commentary on sections

221.   Section 114(1) will enable a transfer scheme made under section 409 of the GLA Act to exempt LRT's/LUL's contracts from section 412(3) of that Act, and subsection (4) ensures that the exemption will continue to apply where a subsequent transfer scheme is made under paragraph 2(3) of Schedule 12 to that Act. Subsection (2) will enable Transport for London to exempt contracts from paragraph 2(3) of Schedule 12 to that Act. These parts of the GLA Act may otherwise frustrate parts of contracts made by LRT/LUL or Transport for London, such as change of control provisions, which are designed to operate when transfer schemes are made.

222.   Subsection (3) ensures that London Transport and Transport for London, when exempting contracts from section 412(3) of the GLA Act or paragraph 2(3) of Schedule 12 to that Act, may exempt either all the contracts being transferred, or a specific contract, or particular provisions within those contracts.

223.   Section 114(5) enables provisions of the GLA Act which relate to the insolvency and

winding up of a London Underground public private partnership company, and the return of its assets to the public sector, to come into effect before the transfer of London Underground to Transport for London. The GLA Act did not contemplate the possibility of a significant delay between completion of a PPP agreement and transfer of the London Underground to Transport for London. Section 114(6) will allow the insolvency provisions in sections 220 to 224 of the GLA Act to come into force before the transfer of LUL to Transport for London.

224.   Section 115 enables the London Underground PPP Arbiter to receive information from those statutory bodies to whom he is permitted by the GLA Act to release information. The GLA Act allows the PPP Arbiter to release information about specific individuals and their businesses to regulators of other industries to help them fulfil their statutory functions, but without section 115 it does not allow him to receive such information from them.

Public sector financial and manpower cost

225.   The railways in London measures will not require any additional public expenditure over and above that envisaged in LRT's/LUL's contracts, or entail any additional public sector manpower burden.

Human Rights assessment

226.   The amendments to the Greater London Authority Act 1999 do not appear to involve any human rights implications, so the provisions of the Act concerning the Greater London Authority Act 1999 are compatible with the Convention.

Part 7 – General

Section 116: Schedules 1 & 4: sequestration, &c. in Scotland

227.   Section 116 sets out the circumstances in which liability to removal from membership of the Office of Rail Regulation and ineligibility for membership of the British Transport Police Authority on grounds of bankruptcy in Scotland shall cease.

Section 120: Commencement

228.   Subsection (3) provides for transitional arrangements to be made if commencement of the Office of Rail Regulation takes place before legislation establishing bankruptcy restrictions orders has come into force. This is relevant because paragraph 2(c) of Schedule 1 allows an Office member to be dismissed if he is the subject of a bankruptcy restrictions order (or an interim order). These new orders are provided for in the Enterprise Act 2002, but the relevant provisions of that Act are not yet in force.

SUMMARY OF THE REGULATORY APPRAISAL

Rail Accident Investigation Branch

229.   Assessment has indicated that the likely safety benefits from the Rail Accident

Investigation Branch can be expected to cover the expected costs. RAIB will have an estimated base case cost over the period 2003-2012 of £17m. This will be borne by the existing budget of the Department for Transport, in the same manner as is done with the Air and Marine Accident Investigation Branches (AAIB & MAIB). A $2^1/_2$% reduction in numbers of accidents over 2003-2012 would yield a £22m benefit in the base case.

Office of Rail Regulation

230.　The Better Regulation Task Force report 'Economic Regulators' (July 2001) favoured regulatory boards on the lines of a public limited company with a combination of executive and non-executive members. This was seen as providing a wide range of expertise, greater continuity and more transparent accountability. These benefits have been widely accepted and rail is the only remaining utility regulator that is not a board or in the process of being made into a board.

231.　There will be additional costs for the appointment of additional non-executive members to a Regulatory Board of the Office of Rail Regulation. This would be recovered at least in part from the regulated industry, to some extent offset indirectly by increases in public subsidy. The extra costs would probably be less than £200k, which is less than a 1.5% increase in the costs of the regulator, and compares with annual income of about £3.9 billion for Network Rail alone.

British Transport Police

232.　The additional administrative cost of a police authority of 13 members over the cost of the current Committee of 9 is estimated at £50,000 per annum in the context of a BTP's total annual budget of £136 million, and will be funded by the industry. In view of the negligible impact of these measures, no regulatory impact assessment is required or appropriate.

Shipping and aviation: Alcohol and drugs

233.　There is a clear but unquantifiable risk to passengers, crew and the general public from aviation and shipping incidents caused by the inappropriate operation, control or maintenance of vessels or aircraft by persons under the influence of drink or drugs. The introduction of alcohol limits in the marine and aviation sectors will help to reduce this risk by deterring personnel from being impaired through alcohol or drugs whilst on duty and hence act to improve safety to the benefit of users and travelling passengers alike. The alcohol limit will ensure that crews and other persons carrying out specified safety-critical aviation and maritime functions retain the necessary mental and physical skills to manoeuvre vessels and aircraft, in a safe and controlled manner. This will mean savings in terms of pollution prevention (clear-up costs, effects on wildlife etc.); saving damage to or loss of vessels or aircraft; and preventing injury or even loss of life. If it should lead to material reductions in accident numbers, then insurance premiums may possibly decrease in real terms (i.e. no or a small increase versus an increase in inflation).

234.　While the introduction of an alcohol limit and alcohol/drugs testing should not have any direct financial implications for the marine and aviation industries, it is possible that delays may occur if crews are made to wait to be tested. Such delays will however be kept to a minimum by the use of screening equipment to analyse initial breath samples at the scene. In addition, testing will only be carried out where an officer has reasonable suspicion that one of the offences under the new legislation has been, or is being, committed. Testing and enforcing an alcohol limit on marine and aviation personnel will place an increased burden on police resources, but this is expected to be largely offset by use of existing resources. In the aviation sector, there will be a small additional implementation cost involved in the necessary modification of existing police screening equipment to indicate a "fail" at the lower aviation limit. The number of prosecutions resulting from the new legislation is expected to be small, but will involve additional policy costs to the courts. These are also expected to be small and to an extent offset by fines.

International Carriage by Rail

235. The new COTIF text provides an updated and expanded set of uniform rules for international rail passenger and freight carriage. In general the changes will have limited impact on the UK rail industry as they broadly bring the Convention provisions into line with existing UK practice. In particular, the new uniform rules on technical acceptance and standards for railway equipment will not impose any new burdens on operators in EC Member States, as the new COTIF includes provisions to ensure that the EC law on these matters prevails. However, the new COTIF text does increase the minimum levels of compensation for certain incidents throughout all signatory states. This will be of benefit to UK citizens making international rail journeys.

Greater London Authority

236. The amendments to the Greater London Authority Act 1999 are designed solely to achieve Parliament's original intentions as regards the Act, correcting some unforeseen consequences of how the Act and the London Underground Public Private Partnership (PPP) contracts would operate together. The planned amendments would ensure that Tube assets return to the public sector in the highly unlikely event of a PPP company defaulting on a contract before London Underground transfers to Transport for London. They would also ensure that the GLA Act does not restrict certain provisions included in the PPP contracts or a guarantee given to providers of finance by London Regional Transport. The amendments will permit the PPP contracts and the guarantee to operate as intended. There would be no other effect on businesses, charities or the voluntary sector.

Hansard references

237.   The following table sets out the dates and Hansard references for each

Stage of Bill	Date	Hansard Reference
House of Commons		
Introduction	14 January 2003	Vol. 397, Col 552
2nd Reading	28 January 2003	Vol. 398, Cols 763-830
Committee Stage	4, 6, 11, 13, 25 & 27 February; 4, 6 & 11 March 2003	Hansard Standing Committee D
Report Stage	31 March 2003	Vol. 402, Cols 669-757
3rd Reading	31 March 2003	Vol. 402, Cols 757-764
Consideration of Lords Amendments	8th July 2003	Vol. 408, Cols 1103-1115
House of Lords		
Introduction	1st April 2003	Vol. 646, Col 1247
2nd Reading	1st May 2003	Vol. 647, Cols 799-831
Committee Stage	19 May 2003	Vol. 648, Cols GC1-GC 54
	5th June 2003	Vol. 648, Cols GC249-308
Report Stage	19th June 2003	Vol. 649, Cols 973-1014
3rd Reading	3rd July 2003	Vol. 650, Cols 1033-1045
Consideration of Commons Amendments	10th July 2003	Vol. 651, Cols 429-433
Royal Assent		
Royal Assent	10th July 2003	House of Lords Hansard Vol 651 Col 470 House of Commons Hansard Vol 408 Col 1429

Printed in the UK by The Stationery Office Limited
under the authority and superintendence of Carol Tullo, Controller of
Her Majesty's Stationery Office and Queen's Printer of Acts of Parliament